W9-CAY-779

Ellington Middle School
Library Media Center

THE LIBRARY OF
AMERICAN
LIVES AND TIMES™

ROBERT E. LEE

Legendary Commander of the Confederacy

Paul Christopher Anderson
Clemson University

The Rosen Publishing Group's
PowerPlus Books™
New York

To Marilyn Bradford, a wonderful teacher

Published in 2003 by The Rosen Publishing Group, Inc.
29 East 21st Street, New York, NY 10010

First Edition

*Editor's Note: All quotations have been reproduced as they appeared in
the letters and diaries from which they were borrowed. No correction was
made to the inconsistent spelling that was common in that time period.*

Library of Congress Cataloging-in-Publication Data

Anderson, Paul Christopher.
Robert E. Lee : legendary commander of the Confederacy / Paul
Christopher Anderson.— 1st ed.
  p. cm. — (The Library of American lives and times)
Includes bibliographical references and index.
ISBN 0-8239-5748-9 (lib. bdg.)
1. Lee, Robert E. (Robert Edward), 1807–1870—Juvenile literature.
2. Generals—Confederate States of America—Biography—Juvenile
literature. 3. Confederate States of America. Army—Biography—
Juvenile literature. 4. United States—History—Civil War, 1861–1865—
Campaigns—Juvenile literature. [1. Lee, Robert E. (Robert Edward),
1807–1870. 2. Generals. 3. Confederate States of America. 4. United
States—History—Civil War, 1861–1865.] I. Title. II. Series.
  E467.1.L4 A79 2003
  973.7'3'092—dc21
                                                          2001006966

Manufactured in the United States of America

CONTENTS

1. A Decision at Arlington House

Alone in the early morning stillness in a mansion called Arlington, just west of Washington, D.C., Robert Edward Lee of the U.S. Army wrote a letter of twenty words. The handwriting was that of a polished gentleman. The words were those of a soldier who had spent most of his life defending the United States of America. "Sir," Lee addressed the secretary of war, "I have the honor to tender the resignation of my commission as Colonel of the 1st Regiment of Cavalry." For Lee, they were crushing, heartbreaking, devastating words. The sun had not even come up yet on Saturday, April 20, 1861, and it was already one of the saddest days of his life.

Lee was worried and anxious, as were many Americans. However, that April, at least as many Americans were filled with excitement and energy. In the five months before Lee's lonely night at Arlington,

---

Opposite: In this famous 1838 image by William Edward West, Robert E. Lee wears the dress uniform of a first lieutenant of engineers in the U.S. Army.

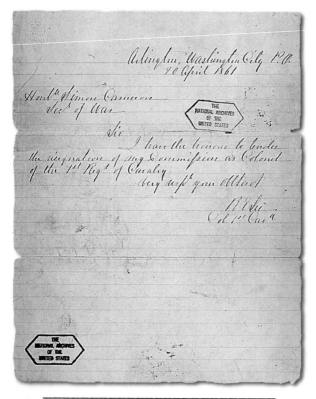

On April 20, 1861, Lee sent this letter to Secretary of War Simon Cameron, resigning as colonel of the 1st U.S. Cavalry. Lee's decision to resign came just days after Virginia left the Union to join the Confederate States of America.

seven states in the south had seceded from, or left, the Union. Louisiana, Georgia, Texas, South Carolina, Florida, Alabama, and Mississippi had joined together and had set up a new government. These states called their new country the Confederate States of America. They built their new capital in Montgomery, Alabama. The new Confederates even elected a Congress and a president, a man named Jefferson Davis from Mississippi. The Confederacy kept growing stronger.

Robert E. Lee's letter was triggered by Virginia's decision, on April 17, 1861, to secede and to join the newly declared nation. During the next few weeks,

Opposite: This military map of the United States was created by Bacon & Company in 1862. It shows the free, or nonslaveholding, states (green), and the proslavery states that left the Union (pink). Most fighting in the American Civil War took place on Southern soil.

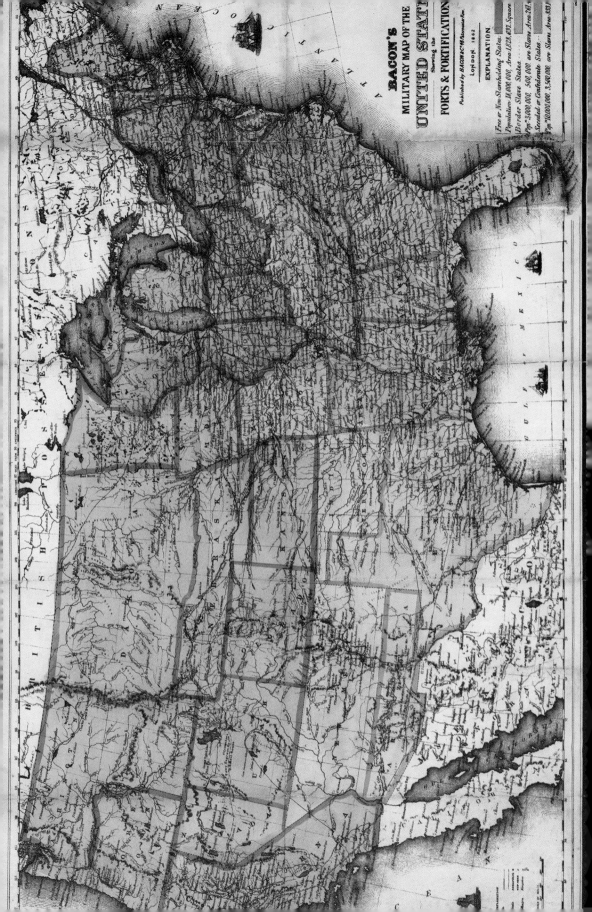

BACON'S
MILITARY MAP OF THE
UNITED STATES
Showing the
FORTS & FORTIFICATIONS

Published by BACON & C.º 48 Paternoster Row.

LONDON 1862

EXPLANATION.

Free or Non-Slaveholding States:
Population 18,000,000, Area 1,328,437, Square

Border Slave States.
Pop.ⁿ 3,000,000, 500,000 are Slaves Area 261,

Seceded or Confederate States
Pop.ⁿ 70,000,000, 3,540,000 are Slaves Area 183,

North Carolina, Tennessee, and Arkansas followed Virginia's example.

In total, eleven states, all of them in the South, abandoned the United States and pledged themselves to the new Confederacy. They were determined to have their independence. Twenty-two states, most of them in the North, stayed in the Union. They were equally determined in their idea that secession was illegal. They were convinced that if some states were allowed to leave the Union, it would not be long before other states would leave. If the United States broke apart, that would destroy the country that most Americans proudly saw as the world's shining example of liberty and democracy. To those in the Union, the failure of the United States to survive even a century as a country was a depressing thought.

Nevertheless, both sides knew what they wanted. They refused to compromise and were willing to risk a brutal civil war.

In some ways, the crisis that led to secession and the Civil War (1861–1865) was a surprising one. The thirty years before the Civil War was a period of intense patriotic pride. In newspapers and magazines, and even in their private letters, northerners and southerners alike celebrated the young United States and all its accomplishments. They glorified the nation's tremendous geographic and physical growth. At annual Fourth of July celebrations, where politicians might give grand speeches, and crowds might enjoy marvelous parades or tasty barbecues, everyone seemed to agree that Americans were truly the freest, most creative people on Earth. At election time, all voters were men, because women were not yet allowed to vote. These men continually turned out in record numbers for that time to cast their ballots and to assert their individualism.

National pride was a strong feature of American life before the Civil War, a period sometimes called the antebellum era. This pride was also deceiving. Even as the country seemed to be coming together, it was moving apart. A number of crucial changes between 1830 and 1860 created greater differences between the North and the South. Those changes set the stage for secession.

The most obvious change in America was the remarkable growth of the economy. Before 1830, America was an agricultural nation. After 1830, it was becoming an industrial, commercial one. The landscape became more urban and less rural. Older cities like New York City exploded in population while younger ones, like Chicago, seemed to sprout up overnight. Roads, canals, steamboats, and railroads crisscrossed America in greater and greater numbers. At one time, most Americans had been farmers. By 1860, more people were working in factories, and more men were working as middle-class merchants, bankers, and lawyers.

Had this economic expansion occurred everywhere in the country, history probably would have been very different. Instead, the boom was concentrated in the northern states. By 1860, most northerners worked outside of agriculture. At the same time, almost 85 percent of white southerners were still farmers. Most of them owned their own land, and many grew everything they needed for themselves. Still, the leaders of southern society were not farmers. The leaders were slave owners, particularly those men called planters, who owned at least 20 slaves. Only one-fourth of southern families owned any slaves in 1860, and far fewer than that number were planters. However, planters dominated southern politics and southern culture.

William Sheppard's engraving from the nineteenth century shows slaves working a cotton gin. The machine helped the cotton industry grow and kept the Southern plantations running, which, in turn, kept slavery strong and added to the North-South conflict fueling the Civil War.

Slavery had always been a fact of life in American history. It began almost as soon as English settlers came to America, and it was practiced in most colonies before the American Revolution. Slavery was even protected by the U.S. Constitution. However, after the American Revolution, during which Americans had declared that "all men were created equal," many northern states began abolishing slavery. Feelings against slavery only grew in the North as the economy grew. Northerners began to value self-advancement, self-improvement, and the freedom to choose whether to work. None of those values, they began to believe, could be attained in a nation that allowed slavery.

It was easier for northern states to end slavery because they had far fewer slaves. In the southern states, slaves were relied upon heavily to plant and harvest cotton and other crops. By the late 1850s, southerners grew almost $180 million worth of cotton each year. Some argued that the entire southern economy depended on the crop. "No power on earth," one planter proclaimed, "dares to make war on cotton. Cotton is King." After 1830, just about the time Robert E. Lee was beginning his career in the U.S. Army, southerners became even more determined to sustain their way of life. They sensed that the development of an industrial economy threatened them. They also sensed that more and more northerners were becoming angrier about slavery. Once, even southerners had thought that slavery was wrong. They had called it "a necessary evil." After 1830, they began to rationalize it as right and good, for themselves and for the black people they held in bondage.

One more element created sectional animosity, or tension between the North and the South. That element was the nation's geographic expansion. In 1789, the year in which the Constitution was ratified, the country's territory did not extend past the Mississippi River. In 1803, America doubled in size after the Louisiana Purchase. Victory in the Mexican War (1846–1848) pushed the borders of the United States all the way to the Pacific Ocean. The arguments that led to the Civil War drew their force from expansion. Northerners wanted to keep slavery out of the new territory, but southerners wanted the right to spread it. In 1820, the Missouri Compromise had settled these arguments without war. After 1848, Americans began to disagree over what to do with the territory taken from Mexico, and violence became more likely.

When the break came in 1861, it found Robert E. Lee at Arlington. He did not want either secession or war. However, he felt trapped between loyalty to Virginia and loyalty to the United States. He signed his letter of resignation from the U.S. Army, sealed it, and prepared to send it on its way.

2. A First Family Falls from Grace

It is difficult to predict which people will have great influence. Still, many people in antebellum Virginia might reasonably have expected remarkable achievements from Robert E. Lee. He was born at Stratford, the historic home of the Lee family, in Westmoreland County, Virginia, on January 19, 1807. Robert was the youngest son of Ann Carter Lee and Henry Lee. Ann and Henry had five children altogether, but the first, Algernon, died in infancy.

Stratford Hall was built in Virginia by Thomas Lee in the late 1730s. This photograph of Stratford was taken between 1920 and 1950.

Young Robert was a Lee, and in Virginia the Lees were people of wealth and influence. They were one family of a select few who were counted among the first families of Virginia. This meant that the Lees were among the first to arrive in Virginia, when it was a colony, and also that the Lees were among the elite in social status. On his father's side, Robert was descended from a long line of gentlemen planters, slave owners, lawyers, and statesmen who wielded considerable power in Virginia's political and social circles. His mother's family was perhaps even more aristocratic. Ann Carter Lee's great-grandfather was Robert Carter, a man who, at the height of his fame in the early 1700s, owned so much land and so many slaves that Virginians called him King Carter.

Henry Lee, shown here in a portrait by Charles Willson Peale, was an American politician and soldier. A supporter of power by virtue of property, Lee opposed Thomas Jefferson and his ideas of democracy.

Prestige was also present in Robert's very own house. Henry Lee, nicknamed Light-Horse Harry in honor of his many cavalry exploits, was one of the heroes and best-known soldiers of the American Revolution. After the war, he had been elected governor of Virginia three times, serving from 1792 to 1795, and had served a term in Congress. By the time of Robert's birth, however, Henry Lee's prestige was passing. His achievements paled in comparison to his astonishing failures in life as a private citizen after the war ended. Henry Lee was a land speculator, as were many of his peers, including George Washington, Benjamin Franklin, and Andrew Jackson. Lee bought property, often with borrowed money, hoping it would rise quickly in value. When it did, he planned to sell it, pay off his loans, and still turn a big profit.

Many early Americans became incredibly rich from this risky business. Lee did not. Worse still, his answer to his losses was to speculate even more. He never made a profit. Instead, mounting debts forced him to sell his family's land, including some of the land at Stratford. His problems worsened. He kept a chain across his door to keep out angry debt collectors. He was even jailed twice. As Henry Lee became more desperate, Robert, his siblings, and his mother were forced to leave Stratford. They could no longer afford to live in luxury, and what remained of the estate, including the house, technically belonged to Henry Lee's son from a previous marriage. The son, Henry Lee IV, soon adopted some of his father's bad habits. His wild spending and mistakes in later life earned him the unkind nickname Black-Horse Harry.

Finally, with his health failing, Light-Horse Harry could no longer take the growing pressure. He simply fled the country and abandoned his family. In 1813, just a year after a mob in Baltimore, Maryland, beat him almost to death for opposing the War of 1812, he sailed for the island of Barbados. From time to time, he wrote letters home, but he only returned to America once, and that was to die. He tried to make it back to Virginia, but his health was so poor that he could only travel as far as Georgia. Light-Horse Harry Lee died there on March 25, 1818.

Robert was six years old when his father left and twelve when Henry Lee died. Henry's spectacular failures left a lasting impression on his son. Though never poor, Robert did not grow up with the wealth that the Lees had been accustomed to having. The Lees now lived somewhat frugally. Instead of living on a plantation befitting an aristocratic family, the Lees lived in a small house in Alexandria, near Washington, D.C., where Ann Carter Lee got by on a modest inheritance from her father and the occasional generosity of friends and relatives.

As a young man, Robert Lee found two outlets for his loneliness. One was taking care of his mother. Ann Carter Lee was often sick. She relied on him to be her nurse, especially when the older Lee children grew up and left to start their own lives. At the age of thirteen, young Robert "carried the keys" in the family. This expression meant he was in charge of such important chores as buying food and managing the family's slaves. His other outlet was school. He was an exceptional student. At Alexandria Academy, he immersed himself in

Robert E. Lee grew up in this home on 607 Oronoco Street in Alexandria, Virginia. Hirst Dillon Milhollen took this photograph of the home in 1906.

Latin and the history of the Greeks and the Romans. In Lee's time, those topics were considered part of the proper training for a young gentleman of Lee's social standing. He especially liked mathematics. Probably the shadow of his father's failures and lack of discipline had something to do with this interest. Mathematics stressed exactness, predictability, and control.

He was not an unhappy boy. He was very reserved and selfless, almost exactly the opposite of his father. His mother, who was very religious, encouraged these traits.

From a distance, even his father before he died expressed pride in his son. "Robert," he once wrote home, "was always good." Still, young Robert was often frustrated. Instead of having a father, Robert had only blemished memories. The famous exploits of Henry Lee the soldier were muddied by the equally infamous disasters of Henry Lee the land gambler, the runaway, and the failure. Friends and neighbors who might have had great expectations for Robert could not be blamed if they expected nothing. Robert never expressed his shame and embarrassment. As his father had done, Robert would become a bold and cunning warrior. With a silent resolve, he determined never to repeat his father's mistakes.

3. A Soldier at School and at War

Robert E. Lee's education, especially his ability in math, was a blessing. Under ordinary circumstances, he might have become a planter, as had many of the Lees before him. That door was closed to Robert because of Henry Lee's mistakes. The Lees did not have either the wealth or the property to establish their son in southern society. Other professions, such as medicine, trade, or teaching, also did not interest him. In Lee's day, southerners did not consider those jobs appropriate for a gentleman. However, Lee believed he could become a great soldier. Southern society did not look down on gentlemen in the military.

In 1828, George Catlin painted this view of West Point, from which Robert E. Lee graduated second in his class. At the academy, Lee demonstrated the leadership qualities that he would show later as a soldier.

This 1827 painting of West Point by George Catlin shows cadets at artillery drill. Besides their rigorous training, cadets had many rules to follow. They could neither cook nor eat in their rooms, and no alcohol, tobacco, or playing cards were permitted.

The best military school in the country was the U.S. Military Academy at West Point, New York. Lee's family name and his father's glorious service in the American Revolution meant that he easily acquired the necessary recommendations to get one of the coveted openings in the school. Robert also passed a difficult preliminary examination that West Point used to weed out unprepared students. In June 1825, when he was eighteen, he left Alexandria and enrolled at the academy. His mother was heartbroken. "How can I live without Robert?" she said. "He is both son and daughter to me."

He was at West Point for four years. The academy did not stress military tactics, as it does today. In Lee's time, the academy stressed engineering. Engineers design things to help harness and apply energy, and engineering requires mathematical skill. Life at West Point was highly ordered, and young Robert excelled at just about everything. In his studies, he was at or near the top of his class in all the major subjects. On the parade ground, where cadets practiced military drills, his soldierly bearing and presence made him the envy of his classmates. In the barracks, where cadets were expected to keep neat rooms and clean uniforms, Robert's appearance was always perfect. The authorities at West Point used all these criteria when they ranked the performance of the cadets. By the time he graduated in 1829, he was ranked second in his class. The other cadets, impressed by the almost unbelievable fact that he had not earned a single reprimand in four years, called him the "marble model." The glow of this praise was lessened by one grim piece of news. Almost immediately after Lee graduated, his mother finally gave in to her frequent illnesses and died.

Upon graduation, the best students at West Point were typically assigned to the U.S. Army's Corps of Engineers. Military engineers helped to build and to repair forts and to deepen rivers and harbors. Lee, then twenty-two years old, started his career as a lieutenant. The Corps was not glamorous duty, but neither was life in the Army's infantry, cavalry, or artillery branches. The pay was low and promotion was slow. Duty was often lonely and boring. Many officers simply abandoned Army life as soon as they could for more fulfilling careers. Worse still was the constant moving about and the long separations from home and family.

In 1831, just two years after graduation, Lee married Mary Anne Custis, one of his childhood friends. The bride, like the groom, was from a distinguished Virginia family.

William Edward West painted this portrait of Mary Anne Custis Lee in 1838. Mary outlived her famous husband, dying in November 1873.

Mary Anne Custis was the daughter of George Washington Parke Custis, the adopted son of George Washington. The Custis family lived at Arlington, an elegant plantation mansion overlooking the nation's capital, where Custis also owned at least 90 slaves. At Arlington the Lees went on to have seven children: Custis, Mary, Fitzhugh, Annie, Agnes, Robert Jr., and Mildred. Lee both indulged and disciplined them. He tried to instill in them, especially in the boys, the same habits of self-control and restraint that he had learned from his mother.

Juggling the obligations of both family and work was difficult. The Army gave orders to Lee and other officers, telling them where to go and when to go there. Despite the hardships of life in the Army, Lee persevered. It was the only career he would know before the Civil War. As an engineer, he lived and worked in such places as Savannah, Georgia, St. Louis, Missouri, and Brooklyn, New York.

This photo of James K. Polk was taken by Mathew Brady on February 14, 1849. Polk served as the eleventh president of the United States (1845–1849).

General Winfield Scott, hero of the Mexican War, commanded the Union army at the start of the Civil War. This photo was taken in 1861 by the Mathew Brady Studio.

Winfield Scott was nearly seventy-five years old when the Civil War began, and no American soldier had been more admired. Scott had fought in every American war since the War of 1812, in which he first earned fame. He had even run for president in 1852, as a candidate of the Whig party, though he lost. When the Civil War began, Scott was the highest-ranking soldier in the Union army. However, he had become so old and overweight that he could not command any army in person, and some people called him senile for thinking that the war would last longer than the ninety days that others were predicting. Scott was forced to resign in November 1861, and he played no major role in the Civil War. He died in 1866.

He was assigned to duty in Washington, D.C., in 1846, when the United States went to war with Mexico. President James K. Polk told the country that the war was provoked by the Mexicans. In reality, Polk and many other Americans desired a war to expand the nation's territory. Whatever the causes, Lee wanted to join the fighting. He had been in the Army for seventeen years and had been promoted to captain, but, because he was an engineer, he had never experienced battle. He secured a transfer from the Corps of Engineers and soon joined the staff of General Winfield Scott, the most famous soldier in America.

This 1847 engraving shows General Winfield Scott landing at Veracruz, Mexico, on March 9, 1847. During the Mexican War, Scott's victorious march from Veracruz to Mexico City made him a national hero in the United States.

Scott's campaign in Mexico was a bold one, and it eventually led to an American victory. Though outnumbered and marching in hostile territory, Scott took daring risks. On the march to Mexico City, for example, he abandoned his supply wagons and lived off the countryside, even though conventional rules dictated that an army never leave its supplies because it might starve. However, moving without his supply wagons allowed Scott's army to march speedily. Scott also attempted to flank the Mexican army whenever he could. In other words, he tried to move around his opponent rather than directly at him. The result was that, when battles were fought, they were usually fought on Scott's terms.

Because Scott did not have good, accurate maps, he needed someone to find which roads to take. He also needed someone to find information about terrain and enemy numbers. This duty, called reconnaissance, fell to Lee, and it was as crucial as it was dangerous. With information provided by Lee and other engineers, Scott's army moved and fought aggressively until it reached Mexico City and compelled the Mexican army to surrender.

Lee had performed his tasks almost flawlessly, all the while earning Scott's praise and continued support. Later, on the eve of the Civil War, Scott would call Lee the best soldier in America. The experience taught Lee valuable lessons. From Scott, he learned that an outnumbered army could win by employing aggressive marches and offensive tactics. He learned the value of acquiring accurate information. Most important, he learned the value of calculated risk. In the Civil War, Lee never hesitated to defy the accepted rules if he thought breaking them would mean victory.

The war against Mexico officially ended with the Treaty of Guadalupe Hidalgo in 1848. The treaty forced Mexico to give the United States what later became the states of California, Nevada, and Utah, most of New Mexico and Arizona, and parts of Colorado and Wyoming. Many Americans celebrated the victory as a triumph of the nation's Manifest Destiny. They believed that God intended for the United States to expand all the way to the Pacific Ocean. However, expansion also sparked violent sectional debate about the spread of slavery, and it set the nation on the road to the Civil War.

4. Lee Chooses Home and Family

The "gallant Captain Lee," as Winfield Scott called Robert E. Lee, returned from the Mexican War a national hero. Newspapers praised him highly, as did official military reports. Lee was forty-two, and by all accounts a dashing gentleman and a charismatic figure. Because he hated personal confrontation, he was also unfailingly courteous. Yet underneath his meek appearance remained a soldier with a hunter's instinct and a gambler's boldness.

Like most Americans, Lee could not escape the growing clamor between the North and the South over the territory taken from Mexico. Most northerners wanted to see slavery banned from the new land. Self-interest more than justice motivated many of them. They did not want slavery to spread because more slavery meant fewer opportunities for them. Slave owners would get the best land, they feared, keeping northerners from owning property in the west. Slavery would also stop the development of a commercial, industrial economy. Unfortunately, most northerners believed, as most southerners believed, that blacks were inferior to whites.

Only the abolitionists, a small but energetic minority of slavery's opponents, argued against slavery purely on the grounds of moral justice. They demanded that slavery be abolished everywhere in the United States, and not just kept out of the territories. They also called for an end to racial prejudice everywhere in the country.

Many people in the United States claimed that slavery could not be profitable in the arid, desert regions of America's Southwest. Nevertheless, southern leaders demanded that slavery be allowed to expand. If slavery was confined, slaveholders were essentially admitting that their way of life was evil. Southerners also argued that the U.S. Constitution guaranteed them the right to take their slave property into the territories. Besides, the South needed to maintain its influence in Congress. If free

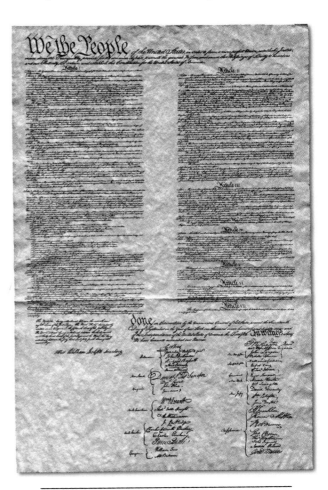

The U.S. Constitution, written in the summer of 1787, defines distinct powers for Congress, the president, and the federal courts. It spells out freedoms for U.S. citizens.

states, or states closed to slavery, were admitted to the Union in greater numbers than were slave states, the free states might eventually pass laws in Congress to abolish slavery where it already existed.

Robert E. Lee's apprehension grew throughout the 1850s, as one fiery event after another added to sectional anger. In the time since Lee's return from Mexico, the U. S. Army had kept him busy. From 1852 to 1855, he served as superintendent of his old school, West Point. Then, in 1855, he transferred to cavalry duty. The transfer meant a promotion to lieutenant colonel and the exciting possibility of combat with Native Americans in Texas and elsewhere on the western American frontier. It also meant that he would be away, yet again, from his family. He accepted the assignment, yet was often bored and homesick. With a touch of bitterness, Lee began to blame northerners for the sectional conflict. Continued agitation over slavery, he predicted, could only result in a civil war between the regions and a massive slave rebellion in the South.

This is an 1850 photograph of John Brown, an American abolitionist. He urged his countrymen to confront slavery as an immediate, moral issue.

Lee happened to be home on leave in 1859, when the single

On October 16, 1859, John Brown led abolitionists to Harpers Ferry, Virginia. There they briefly seized the U.S. arsenal, where weapons were stored. The abolitionists held several soldiers hostage at Harpers Ferry. The event is shown in this 1859 wood engraving.

most tumultuous event of the decade rocked the Union. On October 16, a group of abolitionists led by John Brown attacked Harpers Ferry, Virginia. The federal government manufactured weapons at Harpers Ferry. Brown hoped to seize the guns and move south, where, he also hoped, runaway slaves would help him destroy the institution of slavery in a huge revolt. Authorities in Washington summoned Lee from Arlington and ordered him to capture Brown. On October 18, a party of Marines under Lee's command stormed a small house in Harpers Ferry where Brown and his men were holed up. Brown and several of his raiders were captured, and the grand plan of rebellion did not succeed.

Still, the raid had explosive consequences. Brown was hanged in December, but many northerners began praising him as a hero. On the day of his death, December 2, many northerners wore mourning clothes. Whole towns listened as church bells tolled. To southerners, such displays were maddening and frightening. How could their countrymen mourn a man who had tried to kill them and their families? It seemed to them that all northerners were abolitionists, and that all northerners admired John Brown and wanted to imitate him.

This 1859 portrait shows John Brown ascending the stairs for his hanging on December 2, 1859. Brown's actions at Harpers Ferry, Virginia, generated sympathy for the abolitionist cause.

More troubling was the raid's timing. Brown attacked just months before the country entered the feverish presidential election of 1860. Southerners, already shaken by the raid, were deeply afraid that Abraham Lincoln and his Republican party would win the election. Formed six years earlier, the Republican party had pledged to stop the spread of slavery. It was not an abolitionist party, because it promised to tolerate slavery where it already existed. In the aftermath of John Brown's raid, however, many southerners believed that northerners could not be trusted. They believed that if Lincoln became president, slavery and their way of life were doomed.

Lee shared some of these fears. Yet he had mixed feelings about the southern way of life. Although Lee had either owned or been around slaves all his life, he called slavery "a moral and political evil in any country." Though today we know he was wrong, Lee also believed that blacks were inferior to whites, and that slavery was an acceptable means of keeping blacks under the control of whites. He did not think the best policy was an immediate end to slavery. Lee preferred that blacks be granted freedom gradually.

Because of the sectional crisis, his feelings about slavery were soon tangled up with his other conflicted feelings. Lee loved Virginia. He simply could not separate his identity from the state in which the Lee family grew and prospered. He also loved the Union. Most of his life had been dedicated to defending and sustaining

Mathew Brady photographed Abraham Lincoln for the first time following Lincoln's Cooper Union speech in 1860. Lincoln, the sixteenth president of the United States, is regarded as a person of remarkable political skill and an important symbol of American democracy.

what he considered the only free nation in the world. Like most Americans, he revered his father's generation and its sacrifices in the American Revolution. After all, the Union was the only substantial thing that Light-Horse Harry Lee had left to his son.

As sectional animosity, or tension between the North and the South, reached new heights in the presidential campaign of 1860, Lee's inner conflict became more intense. Several southern states threatened to leave the Union if Lincoln was elected. In letters to friends and family, Lee wrote that secession was revolution and revolution was anarchy. At the same time, he felt that the sectional crisis was essentially the North's fault. He also believed that if the southern states seceded, the North would attempt to bring them back into the Union by force. That meant he, as an officer in the U.S. Army, would have to help carry out that mission. He found that possibility equally horrifying. He determined to follow the lead of Virginia. Whatever course the state decided on, he would follow it.

Abraham Lincoln did win the election of 1860. Beginning with South Carolina in December, the seven states of the Deep South did secede. For the time being, Virginia stayed in the Union as the Deep South formed the Confederacy. On April 12, 1861, Confederates in South Carolina fired on Fort Sumter, a fort occupied by U.S. troops in Charleston Harbor. Two days later, soldiers at Fort Sumter surrendered. The next day, on April 15,

The North-South conflict erupted in violence on April 12, 1861, when Confederate guns fired at Fort Sumter in Charleston Harbor. The Confederate attack on Union troops at Fort Sumter was the opening battle of the American Civil War.

Lincoln asked the remaining states to provide volunteers for a 75,000-man army to suppress the Confederate rebellion. The decision to use force prompted Virginia to secede in a secret vote on April 17.

Lee had spent most of his time after the Brown raid on frontier duty in Texas. In April 1861, he was home on leave. The day after Virginia's secret secession, Lee was summoned to an important meeting in Washington, D.C., with his old mentor, Winfield Scott. Scott made Lee an astonishing offer: Would Lee lead the army that Lincoln was assembling to put down the Confederate rebellion? Accepting the offer would have brought Lee to the height of a long and often difficult career. Still, his answer was quick, decided, and firm. He would not. He could not. Had Lee accepted Scott's offer, the Civil War might have been drastically different. However, waging a war against the South, his home, to preserve the Union, as Lee had said earlier, did not appeal to him at all.

The next day, April 19, Virginia's action became public knowledge. It was one thing for Lee to decline command of Lincoln's volunteer army. It was another thing to be in the U.S. Army when Virginia was out of the Union. Lee's mind on this point, though anguished, was already made up. After midnight, he sat down at Arlington and wrote his short, sad letter of resignation to the secretary of war. "With all my devotion to the Union," he soon explained in a letter to his sister, "and the feeling of loyalty and duty of an American citizen, I have not been able to make up my mind to raise my hand against my relatives, my children, my home." To his brother, he wrote on April 20, "Save in defense of my native state, I have no desire ever again to draw my sword."

5. Lee's Early Career as a Confederate Leader

Robert E. Lee's remark to his brother was genuine, but Lee was being sentimental rather than completely truthful. He already knew that Virginia had seceded. He knew that Lincoln was planning to restore the Union by force. In other words, he knew even as he wrote that he would be asked to draw his sword in defense of his native state.

Almost immediately, the call came. Lee was one of the most experienced soldiers in America. He certainly was the most famous soldier in Virginia. On April 22, 1861, after journeying to Richmond, he met with Governor John Letcher. Letcher asked Lee to lead Virginia's military forces. This time, Lee said yes. As events turned out, he never spent another night at his Arlington home.

Governor John Letcher was photographed between 1860 and 1865 by the Mathew Brady Studio.

For Lee, as it was for almost everyone involved in it, the Civil War was the hardest four years of his life. The actual fighting was still months away in the spring of 1861, but Lee's workload was difficult. He had to make plans to defend Virginia. He had to make sure that the thousands of men who volunteered to fight for Virginia were trained and fed. When the time came, he had to make sure that Virginian troops were transferred smoothly into the Confederate service. The pressures were already staggering. They became enormous when Southern leaders decided to thank Virginia for joining the Confederacy and moved the capital from Montgomery, Alabama, to Richmond, Virginia. Richmond would have been a Union target even had it not become the capital, but the stakes had just been raised. Virginia would become the central battleground of the Civil War.

Lee worked with a seriousness of purpose that might have surprised many Confederates. Most Southerners, like most Northerners, did not believe the Civil War would last for more than ninety days. The common perception was that one big battle would settle the whole thing. Lee, however, expected a "long and bloody war," said an aide who worked with him. Those who proclaimed otherwise, Lee said, were being foolish.

Some of the Southern talk about a ninety-day war was hollow hope. If the war became long and ugly, the North had significant advantages, ones that could be

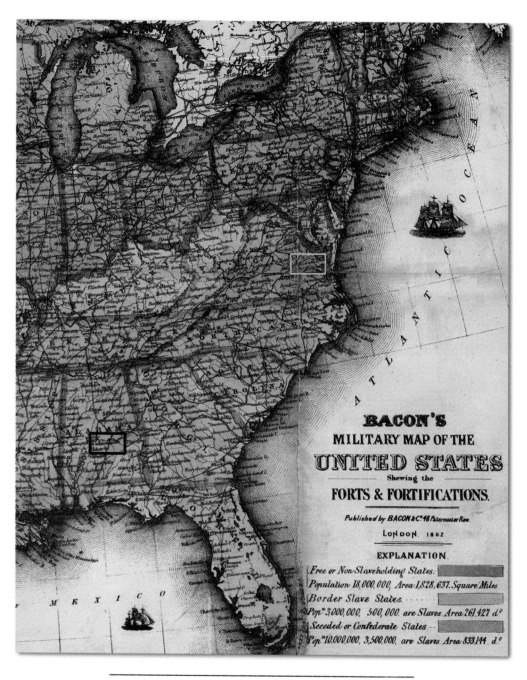

When Virginia left the Union in 1861, the Confederate capital was moved from Montgomery, Alabama, to Richmond, Virginia. In this 1862 military map of the United States, Richmond is highlighted in yellow and Montgomery is outlined in blue. A military map helps army commanders plan how and where to position their troops.

fatal to Southerners. The Union could replace men lost on the battlefield. Of the twenty-two million people in the North in 1861, about four million were men of military age. The Union could feed its armies, thanks to the abundant farms of the Midwest. It could supply them with clothes and arms, thanks to its vast industrial capability. The Confederacy suffered by comparison. Of the nine million whites who lived in the South, only one million were men of military age.

Though the Confederacy could feed its armies, it would have a harder time manufacturing clothes, making firearms, and repairing crucial railroad tracks. Massachusetts alone produced as many manufactured goods as did all the Southern states combined.

Lee's job as commander of Virginia's forces ended on May 29, 1861, when Confederate president Jefferson Davis and the rest of his government arrived in Richmond. The Virginia troops were transferred into the service of the Confederacy, leaving Lee

This portrait of General Pierre Gustave Toutant Beauregard was created between 1860 and 1865. Beauregard led Confederate troops throughout the Civil War.

without a command. The army in Virginia was instead directed by General Pierre Gustave Toutant Beauregard, who supervised the surrender of Fort Sumter and immediately became the Confederacy's most admired figure. Lee contented himself with a background role. When the first battle of the war finally came, on July 21 at Manassas in northern Virginia, Lee was in Richmond helping Davis to develop a strategy and to supply Beauregard's army. The battle at Manassas, or the Battle of Bull Run as Northerners called it, was a Confederate victory. The whole Confederacy was joyous. The North panicked. Lee had been right, though. One battle would not end the war. When Northern panic subsided and Confederate delight cooled, both sides settled in for the long, costly struggle that Lee had predicted.

The year after Bull Run was a trying time for Lee. Although he was gratified when President Davis appointed him as one of only five full generals in the Confederate army, he remained in the background. The commands he did hold were deeply frustrating and unsatisfying. Immediately after Bull Run, Davis sent Lee to western Virginia—now the state of West Virginia—in hopes that he could stop the Union army's advance there. He failed. Next Davis sent him to the

---

Previous spread: The first battle at Bull Run took place near a small stream in Virginia on July 21, 1861. The battle, also called the Battle of Manassas, gave military advantage to the Confederacy. The Northerners and the Southerners were poorly trained for combat in this early battle of the Civil War. This painting was published in 1889 by Kurz & Allison.

Northerners and Southerners often called the same battles by different names. Northerners tended to name battles for the nearest rivers or bodies of water. Southerners often named them for the nearest towns. The first and second battles at Bull Run, for instance, were called the battles at Manassas in the South. Bull Run is the name of a small stream near where the battles took place, and Manassas is the name of a nearby junction, or intersection. What Northerners called Antietam was named Sharpsburg by Southerners. Antietam was the closest stream to this battle, and Sharpsburg was the nearest town. The battle of Stones River, which was fought in Tennessee in 1862 and 1863, was called Murfreesboro in the South. Similarly, each side's soldiers were known by a variety of names. Southerners called Union soldiers Federals, for their relationship to the federal government, or Bluebacks, for the color of their uniforms, or Yankees. Some say the term Yankee was used because the Confederates felt the Union was trying to yank away their land. Northerners called Confederate soldiers Rebels, Johnny Rebs, or Graybacks, for the color of their uniforms.

coast of South Carolina, where the Union navy had been causing trouble. Robert E. Lee failed again, though in fairness the situation was already so awful that no soldier could have succeeded. By March 1862, Lee was back in Richmond as Jefferson Davis's primary military adviser.

By now, many Confederates sneered at Lee behind his back, and, in newspapers throughout the south, mocked him as an overrated failure. What successes he did have were achieved out of public view. It was Robert E. Lee, for example, who in April and May 1862, inspired Confederate general Thomas J. "Stonewall" Jackson's campaign in the Shenandoah Valley, in Virginia. Although massively outnumbered, "Stonewall" Jackson's small army managed to defeat or hold in check three Union armies. Robert E. Lee had urged Jackson to

General Thomas Jonathan "Stonewall" Jackson (1824–1863) was a Confederate officer in the Civil War. Jackson was wounded in battle on May 2, 1863, and died several days later on May 10.

These artifacts, once displayed at the Museum of the Confederacy in Richmond, Virginia, show some of the actual items used by Lee during the war. The items include Lee's field glasses, sword belt, hat, saddle, and boots.

attack rather than to retreat, and in the long run the campaign helped the Confederates save Richmond. Jackson got all the credit and became the most famous soldier in the Confederacy. Lee remained in the shadows. All that would change in late May.

6. The Emergence of the Army of Northern Virginia

We have a great advantage in explaining the past, because we already know what happened. Because we already know how events turned out, we sometimes think that they had to turn out that way. Truly understanding history means allowing for unpredictability. No one's life follows a set course. No event, not even something such as the Civil War or its outcome, is inevitable.

Robert E. Lee's life often turned on luck, both good and bad. Had luck not played a part, for instance, he could have had just a background role in the Civil War. On May 31, 1862, the commander of the main Confederate army in Virginia, Joseph E. Johnston, was wounded during the Battle of Seven Pines. Johnston had replaced Beauregard, whom he outranked, after Bull Run. Davis had to find a new general, and quickly. Since Bull Run, Confederate fortunes, like Lee's career, had fallen. The Union armies had won important victories in Tennessee. Union navies controlled most of the Mississippi River and had even captured New Orleans. Although Seven Pines was a draw, the Union army in

George N. Barnard documented the Peninsular Campaign, which was the name for the main arena for fighting in the east between May and August 1862. Here men are shown near a field cannon in Seven Pines, Virginia.

Virginia was only 10 miles (15 km) from Richmond, close enough to hear the city's church bells ringing. The Union army was on the verge of capturing the city and ending the Civil War.

Davis picked Lee for his new general. Lee was not an overwhelmingly popular choice. Many Southerners in early 1862 considered Lee a failure, and none had any idea that he would become their hero. His first acts as commander were greeted with jeers. They called him Granny Lee because he nagged them about discipline, and the King of Spades because he made them dig trenches. Few shared the opinion of an officer who predicted that Lee was exactly the aggressive general the South needed. "Lee is audacity personified," the officer told one doubter. "His name is audacity."

Indeed, there was no greater risk-taker in either army. Like Davis, Lee did not believe that the Confederacy could win the war by fighting defensively. He wanted to make the enemy react to him. An aggressive strategy might even shorten the war by draining the North of its willpower to fight. The more passive the war was, the longer it would go on, and the more likely it was that the North would simply use its tremendous resources to wear down the South. The risk in Lee's strategy was that offensive war was costlier, especially in manpower, than was defensive war. It was not clear whether the South had enough resources to fight as Lee wanted. Nor was it clear whether most Confederates would support him when they saw the long lists of killed and wounded men. In 1862, following a string of catastrophes, many Southerners were suspicious of both Lee's name and the Confederate cause.

Doubt soon gave way to glory. Lee's first year as commander of the force that he called the Army of Northern Virginia was an almost unbroken round of victories. The Confederacy came as close to winning the war as it ever would, and Lee's audacity was evident the entire time. In June 1862, for example, Lee reinforced his army by

This J. W. Petty portrait shows Confederate artillerymen
with the Washington Artillery in 1861. The Washington Artillery
was part of the Army of Northern Virginia. Artillerymen are
soldiers who operate large, powerful weapons.

summoning Stonewall Jackson's men from the
Shenandoah Valley. In a weeklong series of battles called
the Seven Days' Battle, the Confederates drove the
Union army from Richmond and saved the Confederate
capital. Lee achieved this triumph even though his army
was outnumbered. During the battles, the Confederates
used 90,000 men. The Union army had more than
105,000. Lee then moved his army into northern Virginia,
near the old Bull Run battlefield, where yet another
Union army was on the march. The two armies fought the

This print, created by Currier & Ives around 1862, shows the second Battle of Bull Run, which was fought on August 29 and 30, 1862. To Lee, this battle was a great victory, because it forced the Union troops out of Virginia. Lee hoped he could then drive the war up to the North.

second battle of Manassas, or Bull Run, on August 29 and 30. Again, Lee's army was victorious in the face of long odds. In just three months, Lee had reversed the course of the war. In early June, with a massive Union army attacking Richmond, it looked as if the war would soon be won by the North. By September, not a single Union army remained in the upper part of Virginia.

Still Lee was not satisfied. He wanted to destroy the Union armies, not just defeat them. He decided to invade the North. Several political factors weighted his decision. The biggest one was that a Southern victory on Northern soil might prompt England and France to join the war on the Confederacy's side. Lee desperately wanted to annihilate the Union army. This feeling was a part of his aggressive nature, but he also believed that destroying his opponent would shorten the war. In early September, the Army of Northern Virginia splashed across the Potomac River and invaded Maryland.

Nothing went right. Luck, this time bad luck, again played a part. During the march through Maryland, an officer lost an important battle order. Union soldiers found it and gave it to their commander, George B. McClellan. McClellan was a careful general, so careful that Lincoln himself said McClellan had a bad case of "the slows." Lee had beaten McClellan at the Seven Days' Battle. The lost order, however, showed McClellan virtually everything he needed to know about the enemy, including the crucial fact that Lee had divided his army. Common military strategy dictated that a general never divide his forces when facing superior numbers. If McClellan

This is an 1861 portrait of Major General George B. McClellan (1826–1885). McClellan served as commander in chief of the Union army from 1861 to 1862. This is a detail from McClellan's *carte de visite*, or calling card.

moved quickly, he could potentially destroy Lee's army, piece by piece. "If I cannot whip Bobby Lee," McClellan crowed, "I will be willing to go home."

Lee did not know until later that his order had been lost. Still he knew that something had gone wrong because McClellan, for once, was moving swiftly. Lee managed to reunite his army just in time. On September 17, McClellan attacked near a creek in western Maryland called Antietam. Even more than usual, Lee was audacity personified. Almost all Civil War generals would have retreated in such difficult circumstances. Lee did not. Few Civil War generals would

This painting of the Battle of Antietam was created around 1887. The battle, which took place on September 17, 1862, halted the Confederate advance on Maryland.

have fought a battle in which they were outnumbered by at least 20,000 men. Robert E. Lee did. The Battle of Antietam was the bloodiest day in American history. More Americans were killed on September 17 than had been lost in almost all the wars in which America had fought until that time. Technically neither side won the battle. The next night, Lee retreated into Virginia. Incredibly, he only did so after McClellan refused his challenge to fight again.

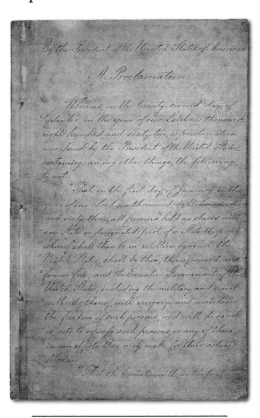

Antietam was a crucial turning point in the Civil War. Lincoln used the occasion to issue the preliminary Emancipation Proclamation, doing so on September 22, 1862. This document promised to free Southern slaves after January 1, and it transformed the war from a fight to preserve the Union into a fight to end slavery. Nothing was

The Emancipation Proclamation was an order issued by President Abraham Lincoln on January 1, 1863, freeing the slaves of the Confederate states.

that clear at the time. With the Confederacy still in full swing one hundred days later, Lincoln issued the final Emancipation Proclamation.

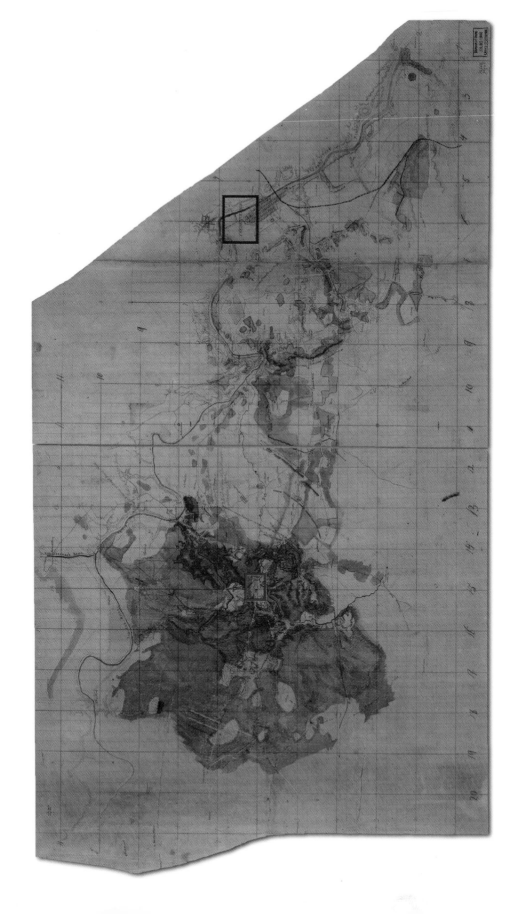

Lee was forced to retreat after Antietam, but he immediately regained momentum. In December, on the heights outside a sleepy Virginia town called Fredericksburg, Lee's army stopped yet another Union march on Richmond and nearly smashed its enemy to pieces. Then at Chancellorsville, Virginia, on May 2 and 3, 1863, Lee inflicted his most devastating defeat on the Union cause. With his army outnumbered two to one, Lee again defied conventional wisdom and divided his troops. He attacked by sending Stonewall Jackson on a secret flanking march behind enemy lines. Though dangerous, the move worked because it was a complete surprise.

Lee succeeded for two major reasons. He refused to be held back by conventional rules, even though it had almost cost him his army at Antietam. He also counted on his opponents to follow those rules to the letter, and they did. They could not understand how he succeeded because, had they been in his place, they would have never taken the same risks. Lee's success was also tied into the way he diligently trained his soldiers and seemed always able to put the right men in the right place at the right time.

Still, the costs were incredible. At the Seven Days' Battle, Lee's offensive strategy resulted in approximately

---

Opposite: Chancellorsville is indicated by a red rectangle and Fredericksburg by a blue one in this sketch of the battles at Chancellorsville and Fredericksburg in May 1863. The map was created by Jedediah Hoskiss at the order of Robert E. Lee.

20,000 Confederates killed and wounded. At the second battle of Bull Run, the Army of Northern Virginia lost 10,000 men. Lee lost about 13,000 through injuries or death at Antietam, and Chancellorsville cost him an equal number. Many of the wounded would recover and rejoin the ranks, yet Lee could not replace his fallen men forever. Chancellorsville also took the life of Lee's most valuable lieutenant, Stonewall Jackson, who died after being accidentally shot by his own men.

The toll of dead and wounded was balanced against important gains. Confederates now believed in Lee. They believed, despite the terrible losses, that they could win the war. More important, the soldiers who had once called him Granny Lee were starting to sense that they followed an extraordinary leader. By the spring of 1863, the Army of Northern Virginia was a supreme fighting force. If the Confederacy would keep his troops well supplied and fed, even Lee began to believe that his army would be unbeatable. "It is well that war is so terrible," Lee had grimly remarked while his battle-tested warriors were slaughtering Union soldiers at Fredericksburg, "else we would grow too fond of it."

7. "It Is All My Fault"

Robert E. Lee did not come to the crossroads of his career in his beloved, war-torn Virginia. He came to it at a small college town in Pennsylvania called Gettysburg. There, from July 1 to July 3, 1863, the single greatest battle of the Civil War was fought and decided. On the hills outside the town, the Union army did what it had failed to do at Antietam. It beat Lee and permanently halted his army's progress. Although the war would last for almost two more years, Confederate fortunes never recovered from the defeat at Gettysburg. Many people have since judged the battle at Gettysburg to be the turning point of the Civil War. Today Lee's decisions continue to be analyzed and criticized. Why did Lee invade the North again? Why did he fight the battle the way he did? Why did he send 12,000 of his best troops on a suicidal attack during the battle's climactic moment on July 3? The

---

Next spread: This painting of the Battle of Gettysburg is a detail of an 1884 painting by Paul Philippoteaux called a cyclorama, or a 360-degree painting. Fought from July 1 to July 3, 1863, this battle is considered by most military historians to be the turning point in the American Civil War. The battle was a crushing Southern defeat.

assumption made in these questions is obvious. Had Lee fought the battle differently, perhaps the Confederacy would have won its independence.

Ultimately all the answers come down to Lee's daring, the same quality that had made him a success. In 1861 and early 1862, the war had seemed like a romantic adventure. By the spring and summer of 1863, these views changed drastically. The war was grittier, harder, and nastier. No one knew that better than Lee, and no one wanted the war finished sooner than he did. Although Lee had been victorious, elsewhere the Confederacy was in serious trouble.

Northern general Ulysses S. Grant (1822–1885) is remembered for his organization and brilliant war strategies. Frederick Gutekunst took this photograph of Grant in 1865.

Soon after the Civil War's opening battle at Fort Sumter, Abraham Lincoln had ordered a naval blockade of Southern ports. By 1863, this blockade was beginning to cause severe shortages of Confederate supplies. The Union also seemed to have its best generals, such as Ulysses S. Grant and William T. Sherman, fighting in the west-

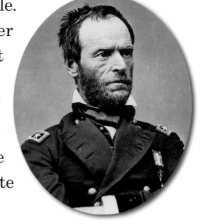

William T. Sherman (1820–1891) was a prominent general of the Union army during the Civil War.

ern part of the Confederacy. At the very moment of the Battle of Chancellorsville, for example, Grant's army was attacking Vicksburg, an important Southern city on the Mississippi River. If Vicksburg fell, the Union would control the entire river, which would effectively cut the Confederate nation in two. Still another Union army, under General William S. Rosecrans, was slowly preparing to threaten northern Georgia. If Rosecrans's attack succeeded, the Union was well on its way to subduing the states of the Deep South.

Recognizing these threats, several Confederate leaders urged Lee to send some of his troops to reinforce the threatened points. Some even urged him to take command against Grant. Lee refused. The best way for the Confederacy to win, he argued, was for him to invade the North a second time. He insisted that if he could win a victory on Northern soil, Lincoln would recall his armies from the Deep South to keep the Army of Northern Virginia from marching all over the North. As he had done before Antietam, Lee also argued that a successful Southern invasion would demoralize the North and perhaps erode its will to fight. His men had been so successful that he believed they were almost unbeatable. Forcing the Army of Northern Virginia to remain idle would rob it of its confidence and fighting spirit.

Lee made his case during an important meeting with other Confederate leaders in Richmond in mid-May. He was so popular that his opinions carried enormous weight. Though the Confederacy was in great danger elsewhere, Jefferson Davis and other leaders agreed that the Army of Northern Virginia should invade the North. In early June, Lee's army began winding its way toward the Potomac River.

James Longstreet commanded the First Corps of the Army of Northern Virginia. He lived between 1821 and 1904.

Problems arose before and even during the march. The devastation from a year of aggressive fighting had stripped the army of some of its best officers and generals. Lee had to reorganize his men before the march. Many troops had never fought together and were led by relatively inexperienced commanders. Also, confusion existed between Lee and his most important and trusted subordinate, General James Longstreet. Longstreet thought that Lee had promised not to fight as aggressively during the invasion, but this was not the case. Finally, Lee's cavalry commander, James Ewell Brown (Jeb) Stuart, also contributed to the army's confusion. During the march, he asked if he could ride his cavalry around the Union army. Stuart had performed a similar move before the Seven Days' Battle, collecting important information. Lee agreed but ordered Stuart to rejoin him as soon as the Union army crossed the Potomac. Stuart made mistakes on his ride and failed to follow Lee's order.

That meant Lee's army was moving into Pennsylvania as though it were blind and deaf. Because Lee did not have timely information, he did not know either the location or the strength of the Union army.

Lee did not plan a battle at Gettysburg. Confederate forces stumbled across Union forces on the outskirts of the town on June 30. Lee's entire army converged there the next day, July 1, and fought a messy battle against part of the Union army. Despite all the confusion, the fight turned out well for the Confederates, except for one thing. While driving their opponents south of the town, the Confederates failed to capture Cemetery Hill. Because it was one of the highest elevations on the battlefield, the hill was a key point. In the late afternoon, in his gentlemanly way, Lee told an inexperienced general to take the hill "if possible." Lee had used those words before, and experienced generals would have interpreted them as something close to an order. The general interpreted Lee's phrase as a suggestion and decided not to attack Cemetery Hill. His decision not to attack meant that Lee's army would be spread thin, on a wide arc, across the Gettysburg battlefield. It was not a good position from which to attack.

Lee risked an attack anyway. Longstreet, who knew him well, later said Lee's "blood was up," meaning that Lee was in a fighting mood, and nothing could change his mind. On July 2, Lee ordered Longstreet to move his men to the south and charge along the Union army's main position on Cemetery Ridge. Longstreet disagreed. He was under the impression before the invasion that the Confederates were going to fight on the defensive. The spread-out position of the Confederate army on the battlefield stiffened Longstreet's resolve. The two generals engaged in a restrained but angry quarrel. Finally, Longstreet relented. Late in the afternoon, the attack began. The ground was unforgiving, and the places in which the fighting was most ferocious later earned famous names such as Devil's Den, the Peach Orchard, and Little Round Top. Still the Union army managed to hold on.

This photograph, taken by Alexander Gardner in July 1863, shows a dead Confederate sharpshooter at the foot of Little Round Top at the Gettysburg battlefield. A memorial was created at this site. By the 1880s, there were many such memorials at Gettysburg.

Lee and Longstreet met again several times during the night and the early morning of July 3. Longstreet wanted to break off the attack. Lee wanted to push it even harder. By most accounts, Lee was more impatient and prickly at Gettysburg than most of his officers had ever seen him. He was not feeling well during the campaign, which might help to explain his sour mood, and he had also been injured in a fall from his horse. Most of all, he was frustrated. He badly wanted the destruction of his opponent. Because he had already attacked both flanks of the Union army, he believed that its middle might be weak. Again over Longstreet's strong objections, Lee ordered approximately 12,000 men to attack the very center of the Union line.

The Confederates fired their weapons in a show of strength before the attack at Gettysburg, but this did little damage to the Union forces. At about 3:00 P.M., with banners flying and the men moving with impressive precision, the Confederate army moved forward. Longstreet technically supervised the attack, but it has come down in history as Pickett's Charge because George E. Pickett, an emotional Virginian, helped to direct the men in combat. What Lee was asking his men to do was difficult. He ordered them to move across more than 1 mile (1.6 km) of open ground and into the teeth of a Union army that knew they were coming. It was finished in less than half an hour, and it was devastating to the Confederate cause. Of the 12,000 men who charged, only about half came back. The others, including an alarming number of officers, were killed, wounded, or captured. Only then, as the men retreated to their starting point, did Lee realize that he had asked them to do more than they were capable of doing. "It is all my fault," he said to them. Later, he burst out to an officer, "Too bad! Too bad! Oh! Too bad!" The next evening, July 4, Lee began the retreat to Virginia.

By any measure, the casualties at Gettysburg were appalling. More than 28,000 Union soldiers were killed and wounded, and Lee lost about 25,000. Never again, after Gettysburg, would he have the manpower to invade the North or to take the offensive risks that made the Army of Northern Virginia such a dangerous force. Lee was so heartbroken that he offered to resign. Jefferson Davis refused the offer, but that did not make the consequences of the great battle any less disastrous. Lee was lucky even to make it out of the North with the rest of his army. When he got back to the Potomac River, rains had flooded it. The Army of Northern Virginia could not cross the river, and for a time it looked as if the pursuing Union army might pin down Lee's army and destroy it. The waters finally receded on July 14, along with Confederate hopes for independence.

8. A Decision at Wilmer McLean's House

The defeat at Gettysburg was all the more important because it occurred simultaneously with another Confederate disaster. On the same day that Robert E. Lee retreated, Vicksburg fell to a Union army after a long siege. That day was July 4. Plenty of Northerners rejoiced at what they took to be God's favor. God seemingly had blessed their cause with two crucial victories on the most important date in American history. After all, July 4 was the eighty-seventh anniversary of America's Declaration of Independence.

The fortunes of the Union cause had improved significantly during the summer of 1863. Gettysburg and Vicksburg were sorely needed battlefield triumphs. These victories stopped Confederate momentum, and they quickened the momentum behind a new Union war aim. From the Northern perspective, the war had begun as a war to preserve the Union. However, after the Emancipation Proclamation, which Lincoln had announced after Antietam, the war became a crusade to destroy slavery.

This 1864 etching shows a caricature of President
Abraham Lincoln writing the Emancipation Proclamation.
It was drawn and published by Adalbert Volck.

The proclamation became effective on January 1,
1863. Lincoln's motives for issuing it were complicated.
He thought that it would keep foreign powers from
entering the war on the Confederate side. He also wanted to use the manpower of black slaves on behalf of the
Union cause. The proclamation, for example, allowed
blacks to enroll in Union armies. If the motives were
complex, so was the document itself. The proclamation
declared that, after New Year's Day, slaves in the rebellious Southern states were free. Lincoln had no way of

enforcing it, though. The "freed" slaves were in areas that he could not control. If he could have controlled those areas, they would not have been "rebellious." Still, the proclamation was a promise. If the Union won the war, slavery would be abolished.

The trouble was that many Northerners were angry. Many of them did not think that they should be fighting a war to free slaves. In fact, just a few days after Gettysburg, a violent riot broke out in New York City, in which blacks were beaten and killed. However, the victories at Gettysburg and Vicksburg helped people change their minds about helping blacks. So joyous were Northerners that they seemed to sense a higher purpose to the fighting. Lincoln himself energized the new war aim with the Gettysburg Address, which he delivered at the battlefield in November. America, he said, "shall have a new birth of freedom," and "government of the people, by the people, and for the people shall not perish from the earth." With those powerful words, he tied the new aim of ending slavery to the old one of preserving the Union.

In the meantime, the war continued. No major action occurred in Virginia after Gettysburg, as Lee tried to rest and to supply his army. However, in the Deep South, Ulysses S. Grant followed up his victory at Vicksburg with an important triumph at Chattanooga, Tennessee, in late 1863. By the summer of 1864, the stage was set for the Union's final push. Grant, who

Executive Mansion.

Washington,   , 186 .

Four score and seven years ago our fathers brought
forth, upon this continent, a new nation, conceived
in liberty, and dedicated to the proposition that
"all men are created equal"

Now we are engaged in a great civil war, testing
whether that nation, or any nation so conceived,
and so dedicated, can long endure. We are met
on a great battle field of that war. We have
come to dedicate a portion of it, as a final rest-
ing place for those who died here, that the nation
might live. This we may, in all propriety do. But, in a
larger sense, we can not dedicate— we can not
consecrate— we can not hallow, this ground—
The brave men, living and dead, who struggled
here, have hallowed it, far above our poor power
to add or detract. The world will little note, nor long
remember what we say here; while it can never
forget what they did here.

It is rather for us, the living, to stand here,

This is a page from a handwritten draft of Abraham
Lincoln's Gettysburg Address. Lincoln delivered this speech
at the dedication ceremony for the Civil War Cemetery at
Gettysburg, Pennsylvania, on November 19, 1863.

had proven himself to be Lincoln's best general, came to Virginia to oversee the North's military operations. Another talented Union general, William T. Sherman, stayed in Tennessee. In May, both generals began moving. Grant's target was Lee's army and Richmond. Sherman's target was Atlanta. It was vital that both commanders have success. Lincoln was up for reelection in the fall. Defeats might spell the end of his presidency and of the Union war effort.

Lee's army was tired. Considering the circumstances, it was also in high fighting spirits. When Grant's army began its push, Lee attacked him in a

The 1864 Battle of the Wilderness, which took place near Fredericksburg, Virginia, marked the beginning of the end for the Army of Northern Virginia and for the Confederacy itself. This 1887 illustration depicts a desperate fight on the road near Todd's Tavern on May 6, 1864, during the Battle of the Wilderness.

dense, wooded area of Virginia called the Wilderness. Though outnumbered, Lee hit Grant so hard that many Union soldiers thought Grant would stop and turn around, as so many of Lee's previous opponents had done before. Grant was not that kind of general. He kept going. The armies fought again at Spotsylvania Courthouse, Virginia, and at Cold Harbor, Virginia. Grant still kept going. The fighting was some of the most desperate and vicious of the war. In thirty days of almost constant combat, Grant lost 55,000 men, and Lee lost about 24,000. Grant could replace his men, and he was willing to use them in battle. Relentlessly, Grant kept pushing toward Richmond.

What Lee feared most was that Grant would pin down his army in a siege. If Lee was forced to defend a specific place, the Army of Northern Virginia would lose its ability to move and to attack. If the war became a siege war, Lee said, Confederate defeat would be only a matter of time. That was precisely what Grant did. In a brilliant move, Grant transported his army in mid-June to Petersburg, an important railroad city just south of Richmond. To defend Richmond, Lee had to defend Petersburg. Though surprised by Grant's march, Lee succeeded in getting his army to Petersburg in the nick of time. He blocked Grant, but Grant began the siege that Lee had long feared.

The siege lasted for nine long, agonizing months. The winter of 1864 to 1865 was especially cruel. Supplies ran

This photograph of the shell-damaged Potter house is part of a series
by George Barnard documenting Sherman's campaign in Atlanta,
in fall 1864. Much of what Barnard photographed was destroyed
in a fire at the time of Sherman's departure on November 15.

low, and Lee's men and horses began to starve. In the
meantime, Sherman's army captured Atlanta and burned
part of the town. Then, in November and December,
Sherman marched unopposed to Savannah, cutting a
path of destruction through the heart of Georgia.
Thanks in part to these victories, Lincoln was reelected
in November. Then Confederates knew that the Union
had the resolve to continue the war. By New Year's Day,
the Confederacy was on its last legs. Many of the soldiers were without adequate clothes, shoes, or medical

supplies. Their families at home were suffering. They sensed that further fighting was hopeless. Lee was the most popular man in the Confederacy, but not even his magnetic leadership could keep men in the army. Soldiers had deserted from the army before, individually or in small groups. Now, men began leaving the Army of Northern Virginia in large numbers.

The end came in early April. Worn down by desertion, disease, and battle, Robert E. Lee's army finally became so thin that Ulysses S. Grant punched through the lines at Petersburg. Lee fled westward, and Richmond, Virginia was soon captured. Grant kept pressing and Lee kept retreating. Robert E. Lee hoped somehow to make it out of Virginia and into North Carolina. Ulysses S. Grant cut him off, however, and surrounded him at the small

Robert E. Lee is leaving Wilmer McLean's house after his surrender to Ulysses S. Grant at Appomattox in this drawing created on April 9, 1865, by Alfred R. Waud. Their meeting lasted for about two and a half hours and ended the bloodiest conflict in the nation's history.

This outside view of Wilmer McLean's house, where Lee surrendered to Grant, was photographed around 1865, by the Mathew Brady Studio. After the historical meeting ended, Union officers stripped the parlor of McLean's house for souvenirs.

village of Appomattox. "There is nothing left me but to go and see General Grant," Lee said to some of his men when he realized that it was time to give up, "and I would rather die a thousand deaths."

Lee met Grant on April 9 at the home of Wilmer McLean. It was a strange twist of fate. McLean had once lived on the old Bull Run battlefield. He moved to Appomattox thinking that he could avoid the war, and now its leaders were coming to his house. Lee dressed in his best uniform, looking very much like the "marble model" of perfection that had so impressed his classmates all of those years ago at West Point. Lee and Grant chatted for a time and then got down to business. Grant could have dictated almost any surrender terms. Instead he followed Lincoln in thinking that kinder terms would make it easier to rebuild the nation after the war. Lee surrendered his army. Grant gave the Confederates badly needed food and allowed many of Lee's men to keep their horses so that they could use them on their farms. "This will have the best possible effect upon the men," Lee said. More polite chatter followed. Then Lee got up from his table, shook hands with Grant, and sadly walked out of the room. For him, as for the men under him, the war was over.

9. "Strike the Tent!"

Although Robert E. Lee's army was not the only Confederate army, the war effectively ended when Lee surrendered at Appomattox. Lee returned to Richmond, where he heard the news that Lincoln had been assassinated at Ford's Theater in Washington, D.C., on April 14, 1865. Andrew Johnson would take over the presidency. A few weeks later, Jefferson Davis was captured in Georgia, in the company of what remained of his Confederate government. Robert E. Lee's mind turned, as did the minds of many Americans, to the problem of how to reconcile northerners and southerners after the

THE ASSASSINATION OF PRESIDENT LINCOLN.
AT FORD'S THEATRE WASHINGTON D.C.APRIL 14TH 1865.

An American flag hangs in the Ford's Theater seating area where President Abraham Lincoln was assassinated by John Wilkes Booth on April 14, 1865. This Currier & Ives print was published in 1865.

This is the only photograph of President Lincoln's body lying in state for a public viewing at City Hall in New York. Out of respect, no other photos were permitted. Lincoln's body was taken to fourteen cities, for mourners to pay their respects, before it reached Springfield, Illinois.

bloodiest conflict in the history of America.

It would not be an easy task. Out of a national population of more than thirty million, as many as 620,000 people had been killed. Although the nation had been reunited, the bitterness of the Civil War would not vanish overnight, especially for the defeated South. Though slavery had been destroyed, racial prejudice remained. Four million blacks won their freedom during the Civil War, but they still lived in a white world that denied them their most basic rights. Eventually the postwar, or Reconstruction, period would see blacks achieve some startling gains. With the Fourteenth and Fifteenth Amendments, for example, the U.S. Constitution protected black men's civil rights and their right to vote. However, Reconstruction also saw some depressing failures. Southern states soon found loopholes in these amendments and succeeded in nullifying them for the better part of the next century. Blacks were kept from voting. They were also forced to live, eat, sleep, travel, and go to school separately from whites.

Lee still held the views he'd had before the war. If anything, the war had hardened them. Unfortunately, he still thought that blacks were incapable of using freedom wisely, and that to give black men the vote was to invite disaster. In 1866, Congress called him to testify before a special committee about the problems of the Reconstruction period. Lee said that Virginia

After the Civil War ended, the fight for freedom was not over for blacks in America. Here a soda machine from before 1960 is labeled "White customers only!"

During Reconstruction,
Confederate leaders such as
Robert E. Lee were required to take an
oath of loyalty to the United States before
they could be granted pardons. Because a
pardon restored all the rights of U.S.
citizenship and made it impossible for these
people to be thrown in jail or even executed
as traitors, it was very important. Lee took
his oath on October 2, 1865, in Lexington,
Virginia. Instead of turning it in, a leader
in Washington gave Lee's written oath to a
friend as a souvenir. The document was lost
and not found again until 1970. In 1975,
a full 110 years after the end of the Civil War,
Congress officially restored Lee's citizenship.

S. J. Res. 23

Ninety-fourth Congress of the United States of America

AT THE FIRST SESSION

Begun and held at the City of Washington on Tuesday, the fourteenth day of January, one thousand nine hundred and seventy-five

Joint Resolution

To restore posthumously full rights of citizenship to General R. E. Lee.

Whereas this entire Nation has long recognized the outstanding virtues of courage, patriotism, and selfless devotion to duty of General R. E. Lee, and has recognized the contribution of General Lee in healing the wounds of the War Between the States, and

Whereas, in order to further the goal of reunion of this country, General Lee, on June 13, 1865, applied to the President for amnesty and pardon and restoration of his rights as a citizen, and

Whereas this request was favorably endorsed by General Ulysses S. Grant on June 16, 1865, and

Whereas, General Lee's full citizenship was not restored to him subsequent to his request of June 13, 1865, for the reason that no accompanying oath of allegiance was submitted, and

Whereas, on October 12, 1870, General Lee died, still denied the right to hold any office and other rights of citizenship, and

Whereas a recent discovery has revealed that General Lee did in fact on October 2, 1865, swear allegiance to the Constitution of the United States and to the Union, and

Whereas it appears that General Lee thus fulfilled all of the legal as well as moral requirements incumbent upon him for restoration of his citizenship: Now, therefore, be it

Resolved by the Senate and House of Representatives of the United States of America in Congress assembled, That, in accordance with section 3 of amendment 14 of the United States Constitution, the legal disabilities placed upon General Lee as a result of his service as General of the Army of Northern Virginia are removed, and that General R. E. Lee is posthumously restored to the full rights of citizenship, effective June 13, 1865.

Carl Albert

Speaker of the House of Representatives.

Vice President of the United States and
President of the Senate.

APPROVED

AUG - 5 1975

Gerald R. Ford

Lee finally had his citizenship restored in 1975. Above is a joint resolution granting him all the rights and privileges of a U.S. citizen. The resolution was signed by President Gerald R. Ford.

would be better off if no blacks lived there. In public, Lee generally kept his views to himself. Partly he did not say much because he knew that many northerners hated him and would use his words to punish the rest of the South. Some northerners wanted to execute him for treason. Most scorned him as the symbol of southern defiance. "I am now considered such a monster," he wrote, "that I hesitate to darken with my shadow the doors of those I love lest I should bring upon them misfortune." When he did speak publicly, he told southerners not to provoke northerners and to accept defeat. In private letters, though, he often expressed bitterness toward his former enemies.

Lee had other problems. The war had been hard on his family, emotionally and financially. His wife, Mary, was ill so often that she was practically an invalid. Lee was not penniless, but the considerable sum that he had saved in Confederate investments vanished with Southern defeat. He had to worry about making a living, as did his sons, who also had fought in the war and had to start postwar careers from scratch. Lee also had to worry about finding a home. Arlington had been occupied by Union troops almost as soon as the war began. It was officially confiscated by the federal government in 1866. Lee tried in vain to get the property back. Instead the government used the ground for a soldiers' cemetery. As Arlington National Cemetery, it remains today the most famous burial ground in America. More than 260,000 people are buried there.

George Washington Custis Lee was the oldest of Robert E. Lee's
three sons. Born on September 16, 1832, in Fort Monroe, Virginia,
he served as a captain of engineers during the Civil War and
helped to build fortifications around Richmond, Virginia.

What, then, could Lee do? His career as a soldier, the only career he had ever known, was finished. He was 58 years old and would have dearly liked to live a retired life, but he needed money. For a brief time, Lee considered farming. Before he actively sought a career, a new one presented itself. In August 1865, the trustees of Washington College offered him the position of college president. The college, which was located in the Shenandoah Valley town of Lexington, Virginia, was impoverished. Its buildings were in poor shape, and some facilities had been ransacked by Union troops during the war. Yet there were also opportunities. Lee had

This photograph of Arlington National Cemetery was taken between 1860 and 1865 by the Mathew Brady Studio. The cemetery rests on the site of the Custis-Lee estate, Arlington House, which was the home of Robert E. Lee at the time of the outbreak of the Civil War.

William Henry Jackson took this photograph of Strasburg in Virginia's
Shenandoah Valley around 1892. Important military campaigns
occurred in the Shenandoah Valley during the Civil War. Union forces
took undisputed control of this valley near the end of the war.

been telling Virginians that they needed to rebuild
their shattered state. This was Lee's opportunity to set
an example. The president's job paid fairly well, considering the times, and he was promised a house and a
garden on the college grounds. Lee accepted the position, though he thought the college might suffer because
he was "an object of censure to a portion of the country."

For the next four years, Lee worked diligently to
improve the college's fortunes. Enrollment rose thanks
to Lee's mere presence, but his success also owed much

to hard work. He was as committed to his students as he had been to his soldiers. He reorganized the college so that it taught a mixture of classical courses, such as Greek and Latin, and practical courses in the sciences. He wanted his students to be well rounded, but he also wanted them to prepare for everyday careers. He ceaselessly worked to raise money to repair buildings, pay professors, and to provide scholarships for needy and deserving young men. Always, he remained committed to the future and urged all Virginians to pursue the same goal. Eventually Lee's reforms ensured that Washington College would become the modern institution of higher learning known today as Washington and Lee University.

Still, his hard life had taken a crushing toll on him. Lee rarely mentioned his health problems to anyone. He suffered acutely from angina, a heart disease that probably first afflicted him during the war. As the burdens of the postwar years increased, his health got worse. By 1870, when he reached the age of sixty-three, he had trouble walking for even short distances. He took several trips south in hopes of recovering his strength. Lee made stops in Georgia and Florida and also visited the grave of his daughter Annie in Warrenton, North Carolina, and his son William's Virginia plantation. Huge crowds greeted him in Southern towns, but the receptions only sapped his energy. By the fall, even Lee seemed to sense that the

This photo of the Colonnade Building at Washington and Lee University in Lexington, Virginia, was taken around 1996. This building houses the oldest classrooms on campus. The school, first called Washington College, was founded in 1749.

This portrait of Confederate general Robert E. Lee was taken on
April 15, 1865, just a few days after his surrender on April 9.
Today Lee is still cherished by the South as a military genius
and a person of admirable personal character.

In 1882, the sculptor Edward Valentine delivered a finished statue of Robert E. Lee to Washington and Lee University in Lexington, Virginia. Today the statue is the centerpiece of the memorial chapel.

end was near. On September 28, he suffered a stroke that left him bedridden. He could barely speak. Finally pneumonia set in. On October 12, 1870, in the quiet, silent, and lonely house on the grounds of Washington College, legend has it that he spoke three last words, "Strike the tent!" Then Robert E. Lee died.

10. The Symbol of the Lost Cause

Robert E. Lee probably never spoke any dying words. In all likelihood, "Strike the tent!" was made up by some of his most ardent admirers. The imaginary words, which meant to pack up gear and leave a campsite, still have a ring of truth. To his last day on Earth, Robert E. Lee identified himself as a soldier, particularly as a Virginia soldier. Army life had been extremely important to him, and he always strove to display such values as loyalty, honor, and courage.

In life, Lee was a hard man to know. His reserved silence earned him respect, as did his judgment, his courtesy, and his gentlemanly bearing. His qualities were admirable, yet they were also distancing. Rarely did he ever share his true feelings with anyone. Today we can study his private letters, and they allow us to glimpse his personality. Some of our biggest questions

Next page: This stained glass image of Robert E. Lee depicts him before the surrender. It is located in Atlanta, Georgia. Lee spent his final years as a passionate supporter of reconciliation between the North and the South. Today he is remembered as a hero of the South, and countless memorials and images exist to honor his memory.

about Lee, however, have no answers. When we try to understand what Lee was thinking at Gettysburg, for example, we are only making a good, strong guess. We have no guide to Lee's mind. After the war, Lee thought briefly about writing his memoirs but abandoned the idea. He never bared his soul about Gettysburg or, for that matter, about any of his days in the Confederate army.

After his death, Lee became an even more powerful symbol of the South and its lost cause. In the 1870s and all the way up to the 1920s, southerners had a difficult time understanding their defeat. Losing to the North seemed to mean that northerners were better soldiers, and that northerners had a stronger, more virtuous society. For southerners to believe that either was true would have been emotionally devastating. Instead, they clung to the explanation that Lee used in his farewell to the Army of Northern Virginia. The South was only beaten because the North had overwhelming resources. Southern society was strong and upright. Southern men were better soldiers than northern ones. Had the odds been equal, the South would have won its independence, because southerners were a more virtuous people.

Lee was their shining example. He never made a mistake, admirers said. He was the perfect gentleman and the perfect soldier. He had sacrificed himself for the good of other people. "When General Lee happened to look our

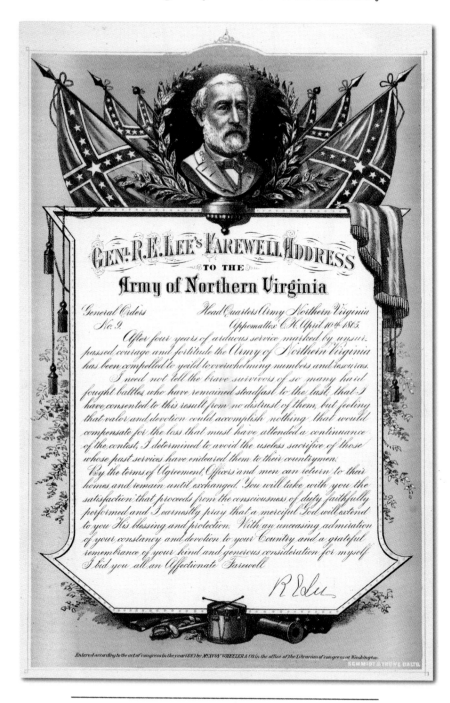

At the end of the war, General Robert E. Lee gave a farewell address to the Army of Northern Virginia, whom he called "the brave survivors of so many hard fought battles, who have remained steadfast to the last." The version above was printed in Baltimore in 1883.

way, he bowed low, giving me a charming smile of recognition," wrote one woman during the war. "I was ashamed of being so pleased. I blushed like a schoolgirl."

Only the South, admirers claimed, could have produced such a man. Many southern boys and even girls were named for him and were taught that his name meant honesty, humanity, and success. In 1890, when a statue honoring Robert E. Lee was unveiled in Richmond, Virginia, more than 100,000 people celebrated in the streets.

Lee would not have been comfortable with the praise. However, he might have sensed an odd twist in it. At West Point, Lee's classmates had called him the "marble model" to compliment him. The Lee worship after the Civil War made him into a marble model of a different kind.

This statue honoring Lee stands on Monument Avenue in Richmond, Virginia. Lee's admirers remember him as a gentleman who held the Union army at bay for almost two years and who won many victories on Virginia battlefields, despite his army being outnumbered.

Adoring southerners turned a human being to stone. No one could criticize him or even question his life because to do so would have been unsouthern. His reputation could not be harmed and neither could his place in history. Because of the praise, Lee became less a man with human emotions and human faults and more like a permanent marble monument to southerners and their lost cause.

Eventually the bitterness of the Civil War faded when northerners and southerners agreed to forget their differences and to focus on the common bravery of the soldiers on both sides. When that happened, even northerners came to accept the southern myth of Lee. The earliest history books about Lee were popular nationwide, and they reflected the common hero worship. Historians, like southerners after the war, rarely criticized him.

Of course, Lee was not beyond criticism. Did the Confederacy really have the resources to wage the offensive war Lee desired, or should it have fought defensively? Lee's loyalty to Virginia might have caused him to overlook important needs elsewhere in the Confederacy. Although southerners preferred to blame James Longstreet for the defeat at Gettysburg, Lee made the biggest mistakes at the battle. When he said after Pickett's Charge that "it was all my fault," postwar southerners should have listened to him. Neither was Lee's character spotless, as Lee himself would have been the first to admit. He could be moody and testy, and the reserved personality that so many people admired often disguised Lee's angers, fears, and frustrations. In his views on blacks, he was very much afflicted by the shortcomings of his time. Many historians today debate these very points.

As long as Americans debate the meaning of the Civil War, Robert E. Lee will remain a prominent historical figure. He is still a controversial symbol. Many Americans, especially southerners, cling to the perfect image of Lee that admirers created after his death. They associate his name with kindness, charity, and goodwill. They admire him for fighting as the underdog and for almost winning against impossible odds. Many other Americans, especially African Americans, also associate Lee with the possible success of the Confederate cause. To them, Lee is a cruel symbol of racial oppression.

The truth about Robert E. Lee lies somewhere in the middle. Lee was genuinely modest and selfless. He was also one of America's greatest generals. Yet Lee genuinely believed in racial subordination. He fought for a cause that unquestionably would have resulted in the continuation of slavery, one of America's most painful historical burdens. However we choose to observe him, Lee remains an influential figure of American history.

Timeline

1807	Robert E. Lee is born at Stratford, Westmoreland County, Virginia.
1825	Robert E. Lee enters West Point.
1829	Lee graduates second in his class.
	Ann Lee, Robert's mother, dies.
1831	Lee marries Mary Anne Custis, a childhood friend.
1850	Congress passes the Compromise of 1850, temporarily easing tensions between the North and the South.
1854	The Kansas-Nebraska Act is passed, reigniting sectional controversy.
1855	Lee is promoted to lieutenant colonel of the 2nd U.S. Cavalry.
1859	John Brown raids Harpers Ferry, Virginia. Lee captures him.
1860	Abraham Lincoln is elected president.
	South Carolina secedes.

1861   Lee resigns from the U.S. Army.

      Eleven Southern states form the
      Confederate States of America.

      The first Battle of Bull Run, or
      Manassas, is fought.

1862   Lee is appointed a general in the
      Confederate army.

      Lee takes command of the Army of
      Northern Virginia.

      Lee's army invades the North and is
      turned back at Antietam.

      Lee wins decisively at the Battle of
      Fredericksburg.

1863   The Emancipation Proclamation is put
      into effect on January 1.

      Lee invades the North again and is
      beaten decisively at Gettysburg.

      Vicksburg falls to Union general
      Ulysses S. Grant.

      Chattanooga falls to Grant.

1864   Grant comes to Virginia to oppose Lee.

            Union general William T. Sherman
            captures Atlanta.

            Lincoln is reelected to a second term.

1865   Grant defeats Lee at Petersburg and
            forces him to surrender at Appomattox
            Courthouse.

            Lincoln is assassinated.

            Lee is appointed the president of
            Washington College.

1870   Lee dies in Lexington, Virginia, after
            suffering a stroke.

Glossary

abolitionist (a-buh-LIH-shun-ist) A person who
wanted to end slavery immediately.

anarchy (AN-ar-kee) Chaos; disorder.

annihilate (uh-NY-ih-layt) To destroy completely.

antebellum (an-tih-BEH-lum) The time before the
Civil War.

aristocratic (uh-ris-tuh-KRA-tik) Socially exclusive.

artillery (ar-TIH-luh-ree) Large firearms, or weapons,
that are mounted on vehicles with wheels or tracks;
also, the part of the army that uses such weapons.

barracks (BEHR-iks) A place where soldiers are
housed.

blockade (blah-KAYD) A shutting off of an area to
keep people and supplies from going in or out.

bondage (BON-dij) A state of being held involuntarily.

cadets (ka-DETS) Students at a military school.

catastrophes (kuh-TAS-truh-feez) Devastating disasters or failures.

cavalry (KA-vuhl-ree) The part of an army that fights on horseback.

censure (SEN-shuhr) The act of blaming.

colony (KAH-luh-nee) A territory of a parent state, with no independence of its own.

Constitution (kahn-stih-TOO-shun) The U.S. document that gives and defines the power of the national government.

Declaration of Independence (deh-kluh-RAY-shun UV in-duh-PEN-dints) A paper, signed on July 4, 1776, declaring that the American colonies were free from English rule.

Deep South (DEEP SOWTH) The region of the South stretching from South Carolina to Louisiana.

elite (ih-LEET) A group of persons who, because of their social position or education, have much power or influence.

Emancipation Proclamation (ih-man-sih-PAY-shun prah-kluh-MAY-shun) Abraham Lincoln's order, dated January 1, 1863, that freed Southern slaves.

engineer (en-jih-NEER) Someone who works with sources of energy.

estate (ih-STAYT) All parts of a plantation, including house, land, and slaves.

flank (FLANK) A military move in which one army attacks another from the side.

frontier (frun-TEER) The far edge of a country, where people are just beginning to settle.

industrial (in-DUS-tree-ul) Having to do with or produced by a large group of people and machines working together.

infamous (IN-fuh-mus) Having a reputation of the worst kind.

momentum (moh-MEN-tum) The force of speed that an object has when it is moving.

nullifying (NUL-ih-fy-ing) To make useless or void.

outskirts (OWT-skurts) The area that is outside or at the edge of a town or a city.

planters (PLAN-turz) People who own or who operate a plantation, which is a large farm that is worked on by the laborers who live there.

ratified (RA-tih-fyd) Approved, or agreed to officially.

rationalize (RASH-nuh-lyz) To offer an explanation or to make excuses for something.

reconnaissance (rih-KAH-neh-zents) Gathering information on enemy numbers and the surrounding land.

Reconstruction (ree-kun-STRUK-shun) A period in U.S. history from 1865 to 1877, after the Civil War,

when the Confederate states attempted to rebuild
their economies.

Republican (ree-PUB-lih-ken) A U.S. political party
organized in 1856 that opposed slavery. In 1860,
this party elected Abraham Lincoln president.

secede (suh-SEED) To leave an organization.

sectional (SEK-shun-ul) Local or regional in character, not national.

siege (SEEJ) A military strategy of surrounding and
wearing down a city.

speculator (SPEK-yoo-lay-tur) Someone who
attempts to buy land or other property at a low
price and resell it at a high price.

subordinate (suh-BOR-dun-uht) A person who is
lower in rank or importance.

terrain (tuh-RAYN) The ground over which armies
must move and fight.

treason (TREE-zun) The betraying of one's country
by helping an enemy.

Whig (WIG) A political party formed in 1834 by a
number of groups that were united by their dislike
of Andrew Jackson and what they considered his
excessive use of power.

Additional Resources

To learn more about Robert E. Lee and the history of the Civil War, check out these books and Web sites:

Books

Clinton, Catherine. *Scholastic Encyclopedia of the Civil War*. New York: Scholastic, 1999.

Freedmen, Russell. *Lincoln: A Photobiography*. New York: Clarion, 1989.

Murphy, Jim. *The Boys' War: Confederate and Union Soldiers Talk about the Civil War*. New York: Clarion, 1990.

Paulsen, Gary. *Soldier's Heart: Being the Story of the Enlistment and Due Service of the Boy Charley Goddard in the First Minnesota Volunteers*. New York: Delacorte, 1998.

Ray, Delia. *A Nation Torn: The Story of How the Civil War Began*. New York: Puffin, 1996.

Web Sites

Due to the changing nature of Internet links, PowerPlus Books has developed an online list of Web sites related to the subject of this book. This site is updated regularly. Please use this link to access the list:

www.powerkidslinks.com/lalt/rbtelee

Bibliography

Connelly, Thomas L. *The Marble Man: Robert E. Lee and His Image in American Society*. New York: Knopf, 1977.

Foster, Gaines M. *Ghosts of the Confederacy: Defeat, the Lost Cause, and the Emergence of the New South*. New York: Oxford University Press, 1987.

Freeman, Douglas Southall. *R. E. Lee*. New York, NY: C. Scribner's Sons, 1934.

Freeman, Douglas Southall. *Lee's Lieutenants: A Study in Command*. New York: C. Scribner's Sons, 1942–44.

Gallagher, Gary W. *The Confederate War*. Cambridge, Massachusetts: Harvard University Press, 1997.

Nagel, Paul C. *The Lees of Virginia: Seven Generations of an American Family*. New York: Oxford University Press, 1992.

Nolan, Alan T. *Lee Considered: General Robert E. Lee and Civil War History*. Chapel Hill, North Carolina: University of North Carolina Press, 1991.

Potter, David M. *The Impending Crisis, 1848–1861*. New York: Harper and Row, 1976.

Thomas, Emory M. *Robert E. Lee: A Biography*. New York: Norton, 1995.

Index

About the Author

Paul Christopher Anderson has an undergraduate degree in history from the University of North Carolina at Chapel Hill and a doctorate from the University of Mississippi. A specialist in the Old South and the Civil War, he has taught at the University of Mississippi and at the University of Alabama at Birmingham. He currently teaches at Clemson University in South Carolina, where he lives with his wife, Keri, and his dog, Mandy. He is the author of *Blood Image: Turner Ashby in the Civil War and the Southern Mind*, a scholarly work published by Louisiana State University Press.

Credits

Photo Credits

Cover: © The Corcoran Gallery of Art/CORBIS (portrait); Gettysburg National Military Park (background painting); pp. 4, 22 Washington-Custis-Lee Collection, Washington and Lee University, Lexington, VA; pp. 6, 55, 83 Old Military and Civil Records, National Archives and Records Administration; pp. 7, 40, 56 Library of Congress, Geography and Map Division; p. 10 © North Wind Picture Archives; p. 13 Historic American Buildings Survey, Library of Congress, Prints and Photograph Division; p. 14 Independence National Historical Park; pp. 17, 23, 25, 31, 36, 42–43, 49, 52, 53, 62 (top and bottom), 66, 70, 73, 76, 79, 81 Prints and Photographs Division, Library of Congress; pp. 19, 20 The Phelps Stokes Collection, Miriam and Ira D. Wallach Division of Art, Prints, and Photographs, The New York Public Library, Astor, Lenox, and Tilden Foundations; pp. 24, 30, 38, 41, 46, 77, 86 Still Picture Branch, National Archives and Records Administration; p. 29 National Archives; pp. 32, 51 © CORBIS; p. 34 Library of Congress, Manuscript Division; p. 47 The Museum of the Confederacy, Richmond, VA, Photography by Katherine Wetzel; p. 54 Hulton/Archive/Getty Images; pp. 60–61 Gettysburg National Military Park; p. 64 James Wadsworth Family Papers, Library of Congress ,Manuscript Division; pp. 66, 75 Selected Civil War Photographs, 1861–1865 Library of Congress, Prints and Photographs Division; p. 72 Herbert Orth/TimePix; p. 80 © Bettmann/CORBIS; p. 85 Prints and Photographs Division, Library of Congress; p. 87 Detroit Publishing Company Photograph Collection, Library of Congress, Prints and Photographs Division; p. 89 © Richard T. Nowitz/CORBIS; p. 90 Virginia Historical Society; p. 91 CORBIS; p. 94 © Bob Krist/COR-BIS; p. 96 Library of Congress, Rare Book and Special Collections Division; p. 97 © Steven Wendt.

Editor Leslie Kaplan

Series Design Laura Murawski

Layout Design Corinne Jacob

Photo Researcher Jeffrey Wendt